I would like to dedicate this book to those I love most. To my parents, Roger and Kristen, whose endless love and support can never be repaid. To my siblings, Camille and Logan, who never fail to make me laugh. To my "grandmama", Julie, who has been a constant figure of love and faith in our family. To my current and future daycare babies, I wouldn't trade the daily hugs, slobbery kisses, or belly laughs for the world! Lastly, to my wonderful friends, I am so thankful for you! I love you all! - Kaitlyn

Introductory Prayer

"I write these things to you who believe in the name of the Son of God, that you may know that you have eternal life. And this is the confidence that we have toward Him, that if we ask anything according to His will He hears us. And if we know that He hears us in whatever we ask, we know that we have the requests that we have asked of Him" – 1 John 5:13-15

Childcare is a beautiful calling and I hope the prayers in this book touch your heart and change your life. Reflection is an important part of prayer, so my hope is that you will use the blank pages provided as a space to reflect, journal, pray, or jot down your goals for the future. You are shaping the hearts and minds of God's children each and every day. Just as they look up to you, I pray that you look to our perfect God for guidance. He has given you a great responsibility in caring for and teaching His earthly children. It won't always be easy, but how amazing is it that this is the path God chose for you? I pray that you never underestimate the power of prayer, and that God may bless you through and through while reading this book.

Contents

Patience

"Therefore, as God's chosen people, holy and dearly loved, clothe yourselves with compassion, kindness, humility, gentleness, and patience"
– Colossians 3:12

"Be always humble, gentle, and patient. Show your love by being tolerant with one another"
– Ephesians 4:2

My mother often reminds me that patience is a virtue. Working with children is sure to test even the most patient hearts at times. Being pulled in so many directions at once can quickly become overwhelming.

Lord, when my nerves are stretched thin or I'm left feeling irritable, please help me to clothe myself with compassion, kindness, humility, gentleness, and patience. Lead me in teaching with love and help me react slowly to anger. I ask you to bless me with the ability to respond to these moments of impatience with wisdom, love, and understanding. When I struggle, let me swiftly turn to You. When I lose my way, Lord, please guide me back to Your everlasting love. Thank You for showing me love and patience I cannot fathom or even truly comprehend.

Discernment

"The heart of the discerning acquires knowledge, for the ears of the wise seek it out"
– Proverbs 18:15

"And this is my prayer: that your love may abound more and more in knowledge and depth of insight, so that you may be able to discern what is best and may be pure and blameless for the day of Christ" – Philippians 1:9-10 NIV

In the present day, there are so many different parenting styles and opinions. When we make decisions related to caring for children, sometimes we are left unsure of the path He wants us to take. Confusion clouds our hearts and we are left hesitant and insecure.

Lord, when I am left questioning what to do in certain situations, show me discernment, understanding, and wisdom. Let me seek your will, knowing that You will show me the way. Help me to discern without judgement, and respect all parental beliefs. Open the lines of communication between Yourself, caregiver, and parents to determine what is best for the child. Let us be open, honest, respectful, and understanding with one another as You are with us.

Love

"Love is patient, love is kind. It does not envy, it does not boast, it is not proud. It does not dishonor others, it is not self-seeking, it is not easily angered, it keeps no record of wrongs. Love does not delight in evil but rejoices with the truth. It always protects, always trusts, always hopes, always perseveres. Love never fails"
– 1 Corinthians 13:4-8

The words "I love you" are expressed millions of times every day. However, a true love, like the love shown to us in the Corinthians verse above, is rare.

Lord, let me love the children I care for like You love me. A foundation of love is so important for your precious children, and some of their homes ache from the absence of it. Allow me to show them love through both my actions and my words. Remind me to shower them with plenty of hugs, kisses, and daily affections. For when I embody a true love, I teach the little ones around me to love each other and to go out into the world and love others. Thank You for always loving us with an unconditional love.

Routine

"He got down on his knees three times a day and prayed and gave thanks before his God, as he had done previously" – Daniel 6:10

Many people develop a routine for their day whether they realize it or not. We get up at a certain time, eat at specific times throughout the day, and so on. Even nature follows a routine with each day's sunrise and sunset. Many childcare facilities and caregivers also follow daily routines. They provide a helpful guide for our day, and keep us on schedule. This can be a great blessing, but routines can quickly turn into ruts if we aren't careful.

Lord, please help me craft a routine for each day that allows myself and the kids to stay on track. Routines help with the stability and expectedness that children and caregivers come to appreciate. I ask that you please guide me to stay clear of routines that can easily become ruts, and instill in me fresh ideas to incorporate into each day. Lend me Your great creativity and imagination as ways to break free of these ruts and make the most of each day You so preciously gift us.

Influence

"Show yourself in all respects to be a model of good works, and in your teaching show integrity and dignity" - Titus 2:7

"Train up a child in the way he should go; even when he is old he will not depart from it"
– Proverbs 22:6

We all have great teachers and influencers in our lives that we look up to. They teach us lessons, share their wisdom, and we show them our respect in return. Just as we have those close to us that we look up to, there are also people in our lives that look up to us. Children often admire those around them as a way of learning how to navigate life.

Lord, help me to be a friend, a leader, a teacher, a disciple, an influencer, and a role model to those who look up to me. Remind me that someone is always watching what I say and do. Hold me accountable and lead me astray from ever worshiping false gods or notions. Let me never forget that Jesus was and is my greatest teacher and role model. Help me to embody His traits and walk in His footsteps. Thank You for the gifts You have given me in discipleship, friendship, and community.

Protection

"But let all who take refuge in You be glad; let them ever sing for joy. Spread Your protection over them, that those who love your name may rejoice in you" – Psalm 5:11

"But the Lord is faithful, and he will strengthen you and protect you from the evil one"
– 2 Thessalonians 3:3

Even the most mundane items can be extremely dangerous if left in the hands of children. Just as the Lord our God protects me, it is my job to protect the children in my care from harm.

Lord, let me not live in fear. Your constant reminder not to be afraid gives me comfort. If and when the time comes to place these children under my careful wing, let us also be under Your wing of protection. I know you are always with me, shielding me from harm. Give me clear thoughts, courage, and strength to overcome times of trouble. Help me prepare beforehand and grant me the wisdom to know how to respond in times such as these. You are my refuge and my strength, I will not be afraid!

Relationships

"As iron sharpens iron, so one person sharpens another" – Proverbs 27:17

"In your relationships with one another, have the same mindset as Christ Jesus" – Philippians 2:5

Building and maintaining relationships with those close to us can be hard work. We must work at this consistently, and relationships with children are no different. While children are known to learn from adults, adults must also remember that there is much to be learned from their relationships with children.

Lord, help me bond with the children in my care. Let me be easily approachable and viewed as a friend. Open my heart and my mind so that I may learn from the innocence, purity, and sincerity these children show me. As iron, let us sharpen and learn from one another. I also pray for the relationships with the parents of these children. I am forever thankful for my nurturing relationship with You. Let my relationships with both the adults and children in my life reflect my love for You.

Compassion

"Be kind and compassionate to one another, forgiving each other, just as in Christ God forgave you" – Ephesians 4:32

"When Jesus went ashore, He saw a large crowd, and He felt compassion for them because they were like sheep without a shepherd; and He began to teach them many things" – Mark 6:34

When little hearts and minds become overwhelmed with big emotions, sometimes, as imperfect beings, our first thoughts are those of impatience. It can be hard to offer compassion, but that is what our Lord asks of us.

Lord, my loving God, please give me a compassionate heart like Yours that offers care, love, concern, warmth, and kindness to those who need it most. Help me overcome my own feelings of impatience or irritability so that I can guide the feelings of the children in my care. Let me be quick to put myself in their shoes, imagining what they might be feeling. I am endlessly grateful for Your eternal compassion for I do not deserve it. I am so thankful.

Energy

"He gives power to the faint, and to him who has no might he increases strength. Even youths shall faint and be weary, and young men shall fall exhausted; but they who wait for the Lord shall renew their strength; they shall mount up with wings like eagles' they shall run and not be weary; they shall walk and not faint"
– Isaiah 40:29-31

The demands of caring for children can often feel endless. The days are long and demanding. There are bills to pay, errands to run, a house to maintain, and endless other chores to finish. At the end of the day, I am left feeling worn down and exhausted.

Lord, please give me a renewal of strength and energy. When I feel tired, let those around me be understanding and considerate. When nightfall comes, help me to drift fast asleep and get plenty of peaceful rest. Wrap me in your love and peace. Remind me to fuel my body with healthy foods that you so graciously provide to us. Let me lean on You in times of weakness, knowing that You will always lift me up.

Discipline

"Discipline your children, and they will give you peace; they will bring you the delights you desire" – Proverbs 29:17

"Know then in your heart that as a man disciplines his son, so the Lord your God disciplines you" – Deuteronomy 8:5

It is natural for children to test boundaries and limits. By setting clear guidelines, we help teach them wrong from right. When they stray from the rules set to keep them safe, methods of discipline help to realign their path to righteousness.

Lord, just as You discipline your children, assist me in using proper discipline to help direct the children I care for. Help them to understand that I am not trying to be cruel or mean and help me choose individual methods that will best resonate with each child. When I must discipline for the wellbeing of a child, remind me to explain my reasoning and use lots of love in my approach. I strive to follow Your example and will always do my best to practice discipline in Your image.

Attentiveness

"Therefore we must pay much closer attention to what we have heard, lest we drift away from it" – Hebrews 2:1

"And he said, Go, and say this to the people: 'Keep on hearing, but do not understand; keep on seeing, but do not perceive' – Isaiah 6:9

Children require constant attention, care, and guidance. It is easy to turn a blind eye on situations we would rather ignore than address. God calls us to step up in times such as these. When we don't know what to do or feel lost, let us turn to God to guide us through.

Lord, let my attention never falter from the children I care for. Help me to step up in hard situations, and to never turn a blind eye to them. Assist me in keeping focused and paying attention even when I am tired, lost, or confused. Let my undivided attention be focused on You, O Lord, and the children secondly. Keep any distractions at bay, and allow me to remain fixated on Your will. With Your holy guidance, I cannot be led astray.

Supervision

"Obey your leaders and submit to them, for they are keeping watch over your souls, as those who will have to give an account. Let them do this with joy and not with groaning, for that would be of no advantage to you" – Hebrews 13:17

Supervising children can often be a difficult task, especially when there are multiple little ones involved. They love to run and play without fear of their surroundings. We know better, and must take careful watch over them.

Lord, when I am given the daily task to supervise the children in my care, open my eyes and ears to our surroundings. Heighten my senses. Let me be hyperaware of potential dangers and hazards. Like a shepherd keeping watch over his sheep, let me monitor these children with Your guidance. Let me never stray far, and keep them in close proximity. Thank You for your constant caring supervision over me. You are always with me and willing to help.

Consistency

"Jesus Christ is the same yesterday and today and forever" – Hebrews 13:8

"But you are the same, and your years have no end" – Psalm 102:27

Some people are labeled as creatures of habit. In the same breath, they might also be referred to as consistent. Typically, consistency is viewed as a positive trait for one to uphold. It allows us to predict a certain expectancy from others, and when we have an idea of what to expect from someone else, we can more easily formulate our response. Children are much the same in that they crave a consistency from their caregivers – one that allows them the ability to predict what may be coming next.

Lord, whether it be in my routine, expectations, or discipline, help me to remain consistent for the benefit of the children I care for. You are and will always be the same. You will hold your people to the same standards today and every day. This helps us to understand who You are and what to anticipate. Please support me in doing the same in my caregiving.

Communication

"Know this, my beloved brothers: let every person be quick to hear, slow to speak, slow to anger" – James 1:19

"A fool takes no pleasure in understanding, but only in expressing his opinion" – Proverbs 18:2

Words are powerful tools that we use every day. They can encourage, teach, and inspire. Words can also hurt, tear us down, and discourage us. Communication is an important part of our day to day life, and misunderstandings can cause great grief. When children are learning to communicate, it can be difficult to understand or comprehend what they are trying to tell us.

Lord, let me be patient when I cannot understand. Let me speak to those around me with kindness and humility. Help me to communicate well with the parents of the children I care for. Let us speak freely, openly, and respectfully to one another. Aid me in being quick to hear and slow to speak. You are in constant communication with me – open my ears and my heart so that I may wholeheartedly hear Your messages.

Positivity

"Finally, brothers, whatever is true, whatever is honorable, whatever is just, whatever is pure, whatever is lovely, whatever is commendable, if there is any excellence, if there is anything worthy of praise, think about these things"
– Philippians 4:8

Negativity seems to drown us when times get tough, we feel stuck going through the motions, or life has us down in the dumps. It is important to keep our spirits up and flood ourselves with positive thinking when we are feeling deflated and empty. Children and even small infants are able pick up on when someone is feeling down or stressed.

Lord, when I am projecting my negative emotions onto those around me, send me an abundance of positivity and optimism. Let me think not about worldly troubles, but of how truly blessed I am! I surrender my grievances and worries to You. It will get better, and I will praise You through it all. Please send me happy, encouraging thoughts that fill me with hope. Let me turn a new leaf of happiness, positive thinking, and thankfulness.

Understanding

"Trust in the Lord with all your heart and lean not on your own understanding" – Proverbs 3:5

"Whoever is patient has great understanding, but one who is quick-tempered displays folly" – Proverbs 14:29

When tragedy and grief strike our hearts, there are things we just can't make sense of. Why do children get sick with terminal illnesses? How can someone abuse an innocent child? Life can appear so unfair and unjust. Children often have a hard time with learning that the world is just not fair.

Lord, I know I am not meant to understand everything, but help me make sense of the how and why. Comfort me when grief engulfs me and I cannot understand. Help me to carefully explain and comfort the children in my care when I am called to enlighten them. Your divine plan is so complex and elaborate, even our wildest imaginations could come nowhere near the truth. Let me be patient and understanding towards these children and others as You are with me.

Respect

"So in everything, do to others what you would have them do to you, for this sums up the Law and the Prophets" – Matthew 7:12

"Show proper respect to everyone, love the family of believers, fear God, honor the emperor" – 1 Peter 2:17

It is often said that respect must be earned and not given or that you must give respect to receive respect. This is not what God intended and He expects more from us. He teaches us to show respect to everyone, regardless of how they may treat us in return. This is a difficult concept for many to master, and we must begin with teaching our young.

Lord, my God, help me to avoid the sin of disrespect. Forgive me for disrespecting You by acting impatient, lazy, entitled, or selfish. Help me teach the children in my care to treat those around them with care, love, and respect. Let me exemplify respect in my daily life by respecting myself, the children in my care, their parents/guardians, and You. Remind me that I shall not do or say anything I would not want said or done to me. Let me rise to adversity through Your name.

Guidance

"And God has placed in the church first of all apostles, second prophets, third teachers, then miracles, then gifts of healing, of helping, of guidance, and of different kinds of tongues"
– 1 Corinthians 12:28

"For lack of guidance a nation falls, but victory is won through many advisors" – Proverbs 11:14

Tour guides are extremely helpful in new or unfamiliar places. They can help us swiftly navigate our surroundings and show us the way. Childcare providers are much like tour guides to the children in their care. Evermore, the Lord our God is the ultimate tour guide to life itself.

Lord, guide me as I guide Your precious earthly children. You have given me endless resources, guidance, and advice if I am only to open my eyes and ears. Let me turn to those around me who have been in similar circumstances for guidance and advice, and let them also turn to me. May we guide each other by Your holy will. Let me help raise children who will one day be leaders and guides in their own communities, never straying from You.

Creativity

"Do you see a man skilled in his work? He will stand before kings; he will not stand before obscure men" – Proverbs 22:29

"Behold, I give you a wise and discerning mind, so that none like you has been before you and none like you shall arise after you" – First Kings 3:12

The Lord our God created everything that is and ever will be. His creativity is powerful and boundless. When we express ourselves through art, music, dance, song, or any other creative medium, He leaps for joy. Children are often perceived as most innocent when they are being creative.

Lord, creator of all, help me to be more creative and express myself in new ways. Let me use the mind You gave me in unique and special ways. Help me to glorify You through all of my creative works. You are a constant reminder that each child is special, unique, and creative in their own way. As a caregiver, let me help draw out the many paths of creativity in the children I care for. Thank You for gifting me the spark of a creative mind, help me put it to good use.

Focus

"Let your eyes look directly forward, and your gaze be straight before you" – Proverbs 4:25

"But stay awake at all times, praying that you may have strength to escape all these things that are going to take place, and to stand before the Son of Man" – Luke 21:36

Even the most diligent adults experience moments of distraction. Our minds wander and we cannot remember what we were doing just moments beforehand. We are continuously teaching children, and it is, understandably, easy for them to lose focus.

Lord, when my mind begins to wander, pull me back and help me focus on the task at hand. Assist me in keeping the children I care for focused and motivated. We ask You to help us concentrate on You. I also ask that You help me to remain focused on why I originally wanted to become a caregiver: I want to make a difference in these children's lives, and glorify You in the process. I am so thankful for your endless love and assistance in my caregiving journey!

Listening

"If you listen carefully to the Lord your God and do what is right in his eyes, if you pay attention to his commands and keep all his decrees, I will not bring on you any of the diseases I brought on the Egyptians, for I am the Lord, who heals you" – Exodus 15:2

"If one gives an answer before he hears, it is his folly and shame" – Proverbs 18:13

It is relatively easy to tune out the noise around us and focus on ourselves. However, we must remember that we gain nothing by shutting out those around us. This is a good lesson to teach the children in our life, as well.

Lord, open my ears and help me listen. Help me to listen with not only my ears, but all of my senses. When that little voice inside of me tells me that something isn't quite right, do not let me quickly dismiss it. Help me be quick to listen and slow to speak. Let me listen to everyone around me. Above all else, let me listen to Your word and will. Help me instill good listening skills in the children I care for. Thank You for always listening to me and being there for me.

Passion

"Whatever you do, work heartily, as for the Lord and not for men" – Colossians 3:23

"And we know that for those who love God all things work together for good, for those who are called according to his purpose"
–Romans 8:28

When we have a passion for our work, it is no longer work at all. This intense desire and enthusiasm, known as passion, is very powerful. The Lord our God has a passionate love for us, deeper than any we have ever known here on Earth.

Lord, help me find and kindle my passions. Let me prioritize what is most important to You and follow your lead. Spark a fire for my passion of caregiving. Give me a ravenous hunger for learning and help me to inspire those around me to follow their passions in life as well. Let me be observant to the passions of those around me and help me ignite their excitement. You give us all that there is to be excited about. Thank You for giving me a passion for caring for Your earthly children.

Encouragement

"Therefore encourage one another and build each other up, just as in fact you are doing"
– 1 Thessalonians 5:11

"For you know that we dealt with each of you as a father deals with his own children, encouraging, comforting and urging you to live lives worthy of God, who calls you into his kingdom and glory"
– 1 Thessalonians 2:11-12

Reassurance, praise, and compliments raise our spirits and make us feel good. Not only does receiving encouragement do this for us, but giving it often feels just as great! Children love to feel secure and reassured in all that they do.

Lord, help me to receive encouragement with grace and give it with sincerity. Remind me to blanket the children I care for in unending praise, assurance, and support for they will remember the kindness shown to them. You constantly lift me up in encouragement and I am eternally grateful. Shield me from using words or actions that may be discouraging, disappointing, or disheartening. Help me be quick to lift others up in positivity and encouragement.

Growth

"For this very reason, make every effort to supplement your faith with virtue, and virtue with knowledge, and knowledge with self-control, and self-control with steadfastness, and steadfastness with godliness, and godliness with brotherly affection, and brotherly affection with love. For if these qualities are yours and are increasing, they keep you from being ineffective or unfruitful in the knowledge of our Lord Jesus Christ" – 2 Peter 1:5-8

Children have much growth to do physically, spiritually, mentally, and emotionally. Growing pains can be associated with advancement in each of these areas. Let us never forget that Jesus suffered the ultimate pain on the cross so that we may live.

Lord, help me to grow spiritually, mentally, and emotionally so that I may lead Your children in these ways as well. When I experience growing pains, show me comfort. Let me always strive to do and be better as I have a long way to go. Thank You for being patient with me on this journey of growth.

Feedback

"Listen to advice and accept instruction, that you may gain wisdom in the future" – Proverbs 19:20

"The ear that listens to life-giving reproof will dwell among the wise. Whoever ignores instruction despises himself, but he who listens to reproof gains intelligence"
– Proverbs 15:31-32

Almost all career paths require some form of performance review from time to time. The best leaders realize that constructive criticism is necessary for future growth. As a caregiver, we should be open and accepting of feedback in order to grow and learn accordingly.

Lord, I realize that respectful communication is vital to openly providing and receiving feedback. Help me to open my mind and heart to this idea. I ask that You be with me in speaking freely with the parents of the children I care for. Remind me to also ask the children how I could do better from their perspective. This can be hard to hear at times, so do not let my heart turn hard or cold. Let me turn to You and reflect in quiet prayer.

Gratitude

"Be joyful always; pray continually; give thanks in all circumstances, for this is God's will for you in Christ Jesus" – 1 Thessalonians 5:16-18

"Give thanks to the Lord, for he is good; his love endures forever" – 1 Chronicles 16:34

We often teach children to say thank you for birthday or Christmas gifts, which is a noble reminder, but the Lord teaches us to give thanks in all our circumstances. May we never stop praising Him for he is so good!

Lord, I am so grateful for all of the blessings You bestow upon me. I am truly not worthy. May you nurture my heart with gratitude and appreciation in everything that I do. May I never stop praising You! I am so thankful for the families and children You sent me to care for. They bring me such joy! Let me never forget to thank You for them each and every day. Help me craft in these children thankful, gracious, and appreciative hearts. Let us thank each other, but most importantly, always give praise to Your name.

Innocence

"Behold, I send you out as sheep in the midst of wolves; so be shrewd as serpents and innocent as doves" – Matthew 10:16

"Truly, I say to you, unless you turn and become like children, you will never enter the kingdom of heaven. Whoever humbles himself like this child is the greatest in the kingdom of heaven"
– Matthew 18:3-4

One can't help but smile when watching the innocence of a child playing and laughing. God never wants us to lose this part of ourselves, and as we venture into adulthood, many people do.

Lord, may I never lose the spirit of the child within me. Let me laugh, giggle, and shriek. Allow me to run, jump, and play. Defend me from taking life too seriously, and permit me to be silly and playful again. You take joy in seeing me happy and I aim to please You. Help me nurture the innocence in the children I care for – may they be full of wonder, curiosity, and lightheartedness. As they grow, may they never lose the innocence within them.

Health

"Gracious words are a honeycomb, sweet to the soul and healing to the bones" – Proverbs 16:24

"For I will restore health to you and heal you of your wounds" – Jeremiah 30:17

It is easy to become grouchy when we aren't feeling well. The sickness overtakes both our body and our spirit. Children often think of health in terms of physical wellbeing, but we must teach them about the health of our mind, body, and spirit.

Lord, keep me healthy mentally, physically, and spiritually so that I can best provide for the children in my care. When my health falls out of balance, I find myself feeling fatigued, irritable, and just not myself. Teach me habits of health and wellness. You are aware, O God, of how quickly the germs and illnesses spread between your children. Help us keep these sicknesses at bay so that we may remain strong and healthy. Remind us to nourish our bodies with the foods you provide and to sustain our minds and spirits as well. Lift us up and heal us, mighty one!

Faith

"And Jesus answered them, Have faith in God. Truly, I say to you, whoever says to this mountain, 'Be taken up and thrown into the sea' and does not doubt in his heart, but believes that what he says will come to pass, it will be done for him. Therefore I tell you, whatever you ask in prayer, believe that you have received it, and it will be yours" – Mark 11:22-24

In the course of our lives, we experience doubt, hesitation, and suspicion as humans. Our earthly reservations are normal in many situations, but we must not doubt the Lord our God. We must have faith that He is good.

Lord, let my faith continue to grow out of my love for You. Steer me clear of any doubt or reluctance. Plant tiny mustard seeds of faith in the children of this world, and allow caregivers like myself to water them. We are Your messengers, Your hands, and Your feet. Let us help each other in our journeys of faith, especially when we face difficulties, trials, and tribulations. Allow my individual faith to grow stronger and steadier. I believe in You!

Contentment

"Not that I am speaking of being in need, for I have learned in whatever situation I am to be content" – Philippians 4:11

"Now there is great gain in godliness with contentment" – 1 Timothy 6:6

We often hear of how expensive it is to raise a child. There are so many "things" that the world convinces us we need. Caregivers can also fall into this trap of "never enough".

Lord, when I find myself wanting more, help to humble me and ground me. Teach me to be thankful for the many blessings you have already so graciously provided. Let me be content with my wages, and focused on following my Cross of Your will. When the children I care for want more toys, games, or "things", show them how blessed they are. Help me to teach them how to be content as they do not understand value, needs, or wants. Let me provide for our needs first and foremost. Help me differentiate between needs and wants. Thank you for helping me strive to reach a heart that is humble, grateful, and content.

Closing Prayer

"I write these things to you who believe in the name of the Son of God, that you may know that you have eternal life. And this is the confidence that we have toward Him, that if we ask anything according to His will He hears us. And if we know that He hears us in whatever we ask, we know that we have the requests that we have asked of Him" – 1 John 5:13-15

Some of you may have noticed that the above verse was the same verse I chose to use in the introductory prayer at the beginning of this book. This was to intentionally encourage your continued faithful prayer life – for "**He hears us!**" I will be praying for you and I hope you will pray for me! – Kaitlyn

Lord, please do not let my prayers end with the closing of this book. Encourage me in both intentional and spontaneous prayer! Let my prayers be full of thanksgiving and reflection. Hearten my passion for childcare, and let me always put Your will above my own. Thank you for choosing me to care for your precious children. Please bless me and all childcare providers around the world. I will continue to do my best and look to You for guidance. In Your name I pray, AMEN!

About the Author

Kaitlyn Stockemer is a 24 year old childcare provider from the small town of Colwich, Kansas. Throughout college, Kaitlyn cared for many children locally and even spent a summer in Australia as an au pair. After graduating with a business marketing degree from Wichita State University and a Masters of Business Administration (MBA) degree from Emporia State University, she explored the corporate world. However, Kaitlyn continued to feel drawn back to her passion for childcare as she finds it very rewarding and fulfilling. Not long after, she left her corporate position and opened her own licensed daycare, Peek-A-Boo Preschool and Childcare, in her hometown of Colwich. As a devoted Christian, she believes that she was called to do God's work by caring for His children. She currently spends her days loving six little ones ranging in age from 5 weeks to 4 years old. If you'd like to see what they are up to, you can follow them on Facebook: @peekaboocolwich. Kaitlyn also runs a Facebook page called Prayers for Childcare Providers to share faith based encouragement. Search @Prayers4CCP to follow!

Made in the USA
Middletown, DE
25 August 2023

37341331R00040